CLARINET TRIOS
18th Century
Also suitable for SAXOPHONE TRIOS and VIOLIN TRIOS
Arranged by
Carl A. Rosenthal

Dr. Rosenthal, a Viennese by birth and training, has had much experience as an editor, author and teacher. After receiving his Ph.D. in musicology from the University of Vienna, he spent years as an editor of the "Denkmaeler der Tunkunst in Oesterreich", the monumental compilation of the history of Austrian music, and as collaborator on the music section of the "Enciclopedia Italiana". Since 1940 he has made his home in the United States, where he is renowned for his editions of little known works of the great masters.

The arrangements in this book are designed to give each part equal importance. This is accomplished by giving each player a share of the melody and accompaniment as well. It should be the aim of the performers to blend their tones so that real ensemble playing is produced.

Contents

EDWARD B. MARKS MUSIC COMPANY

EXCLUSIVELY DISTRIBUTED BY HAL•LEONARD CORPORATION
7777 W. BLUEMOUND RD. P.O. BOX 13819 MILWAUKEE, WI 53213

CLARINETS
or
SAXOPHONES
or
VIOLINS

George Frederick
HANDEL
(1685 - 1759)

ALLA BREVE from Sonata a tre No. 6 for Two Oboes and Bassoon

Arranged by
CARL A. ROSENTHAL

George Frederick

HANDEL

(1685 - 1759)

MENUETTO from Concerto Grosso No. 5

Arranged by
CARL A. ROSENTHAL

Johann Sebastian

BACH

(1685 - 1750)

AIR (Duet) from Cantata No. 128

Arranged by
CARL A. ROSENTHAL

Johann Sebastian
BACH
(1685 - 1750)

ANGLAISE from French Suite No. 3

Arranged by
CARL A. ROSENTHAL

François
COUPERIN
(1668 - 1733)

GIGUE "La Babet" from Pièces de Clavecin
Book I, 1713

Arranged by
CARL A. ROSENTHAL

Un peu vivement

D.C. al Fine

François
COUPERIN
(1668 - 1733)
GAVOTTE "Les Moissonneurs" from Pièces de Clavecin
Book II, 1717

Arranged by
CARL A. ROSENTHAL

Gayement

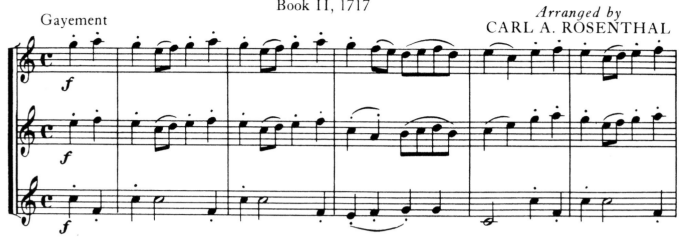

Jean Philippe
RAMEAU
(1683 - 1764)

RIGAUDON from Nouvelles Suites de Pièces de Clavecin
Book II, 1724

Arranged by
CARL A. ROSENTHAL

Allegro

Jean Philippe
RAMEAU
(1683 - 1764)

MENUET from Nouvelles Suites de Pièces de Clavecin
Book III, 1736

Arranged by
CARL A. ROSENTHAL

Tempo di Menuetto

Arcangelo
CORELLI
(1653 - 1713)

ALLEGRO from Sonata a tre Op. 1, No. 1, 1681

Arranged by
CARL A. ROSENTHAL

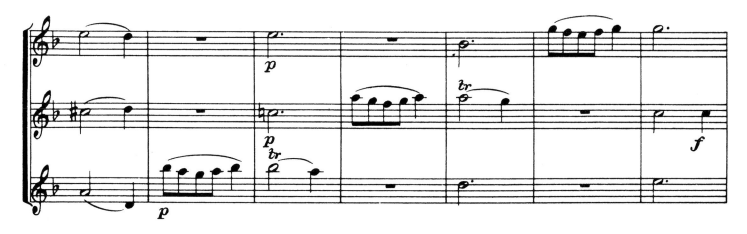

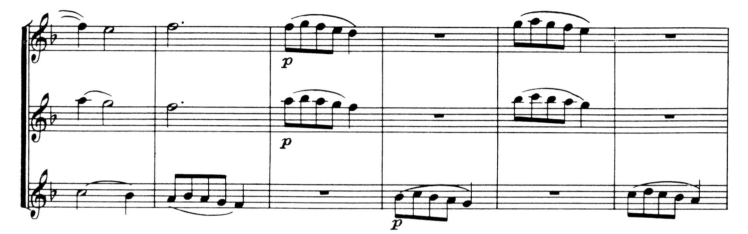

Domenico
SCARLATTI
(1685 - 1757)

SONATA No. 55 for Clavicembalo

Arranged by
CARL A. ROSENTHAL

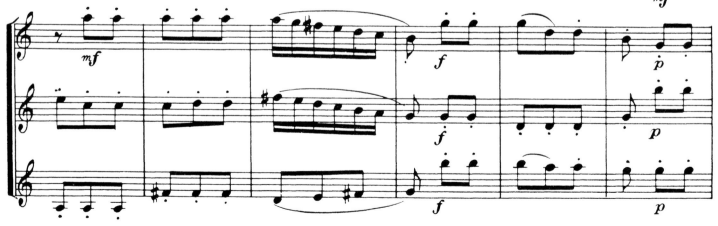